Poems

Michael Boy works as a writer and conceptual artist. He explores the feelings and peculiarities of special people and tries to capture moments through poetry. An approach and a confrontation.

These poems are dedicated to
Birgit, Max and Leo.

Bibliografische Information der
Deutschen Nationalbibliothek: Die
Deutsche Nationalbibliothek
verzeichnet diese Publikation in der
Deutschen Nationalbibliografie;
detaillierte bibliografische Daten sind
im Internet über dnb.dnb.de abrufbar.

Herstellung und Verlag:
BoD – Books on Demand,
            Norderstedt

ISBN: 9783753471549

288 strange poems, divided into several parts.

Incomprehensible poems by and about special people. In search of encounters, self-discovery and self-help as a mixture of words. An affair of the heart.

Part 1

Often you've seen some things from
the front, and then you've seen some
things from the back. Everything is one
and the same. What is important is the
tender happiness and the quiet joy
within you. What do you think?

1. Wound

Do not treat the wound of the heart,
do not nourish the wound properly,
and do not leave everything in the
heart.

2. Alas

Unfortunately,
suffering does not always have a great
purpose,
but suffering always makes sense.

3. Trust

Gain confidence in your thoughts
and turn them into a big picture.

4. Exchange
Exchange fluids,
thoughts and feelings
and solid knowledge,
faith and perseverance and yourself.

5. Hopped off
Over and over
and then run away or not.

6. Short
Facing the sun,
of course,
short and friendly,
although it hurts,
praise the sun,
short and very friendly.

7.   Network
Insulting thinkers for explanations,
finding the right meaning.

8.   Brutal
Drinking the last sip
and being cruel
without mercy is always a good trait.

9.   Promise
Promise nothing
and be the center of the earth despite
the herd consciousness,
come here and surrender.

10. Warning
Gradually the memories disappear,
the accuser is old and thin,
it seems he is exhausted.

11. Reason
There is no real reason
for the accumulation of a large amount
of knowledge.

12. So that
Quite beside me,
definitely want to be there and keep in
touch.

A brief thought occurs to me in between, have I become funnier or more thoughtful as a result of the poems? The people about whom I write and from whom I have received many thoughts fascinate me and captivate me. Stubborn eccentrics without a fixed abode in the spirit.

13. Happiness
Good luck and control
over the worlds,
good luck.

14. Order
Get the order,
execute it well
and be proud of the warrior,
you must be a warrior.

15. Appearance
I came and learned everything,
an exemplary strong guy.

16. Miracles

No additional miracles happen,
what is known should be enough.

17. Frame

The frame has a beautiful frame
function,
which creates hope.

18. See

I couldn't see the sun for happiness
and looked forward to silliness.

19. Slowly
Come to yourself
and be a decent person,
strengthen your arms
and play with your muscles with joy.

20. Twisted
Think,
nod and confirm,
to confirm and think about the future,
be successful.

21. Weekend
Weekends,
end of year and end of life,
find everything effortlessly.

22. Noise
The constant noise in the small head
has become music,
sound and sound,
friendly to all,
be friendly.

23. Pay
If you pay for everything,
bills will not remain unpaid,
gifts are dangerous
and happiness will be a punishment.

24. Abbreviation
Since the shortcut has taken hold,
there is no longer any way to see
burdensome life in the long run.

25. Loaded
Well calculated,
smart, well calculated,
but at the same time clean
and yet a new beginning.

26. Words
There will always be words,
words that describe all life.

27. Delivered
Open rest,
the rest comes back
and everything else is near,
takes almost no space,
everything is open.

28. Finished
Get done,
get the job done
and have fun thinking every day
without thinking.

29. Vanity
Take your vanity
and lose yourself,
fall down.

30. Lights
And it shines the head,
many believe
that they may be infected.

31. Love

Here we should not forget love,
love for each other,
thoughtful love and empty love.

32. Replacement

Replace flowing things,
thoughts and thoughts,
feelings and hard knowledge,
belief and withdrawal,
and yourself.

33. Escape

Escape again and again
and again and again
and again and again
and again.

I have always loved reading poetry, preferably lying under a tree somewhere, drinking a delicious wine or a good beer. I still love to read poetry. I would be happy if you like these poems here and enjoy them. My inspirational friends would be happy about that too.

34. Short

Of course the sun shines briefly and
kindly,
it hurts,
but the sun is admired
and briefly and so beautifully.

35. Network

Fertilize
the thinkers with an explanation
while searching for the right meaning.

36. Brutal

To drink the last cup
and be brutal is the character of a
timeless good character.

37. Promise
Don't promise anything,
come here
and surrender to the center of the earth
despite the swarming consciousness.

38. Warning
Slowly disappear the memory of life,
life is old and thin,
just be weak and stay weak.

39. Reason
There is no real reason
to accumulate much knowledge.

40. Like this
I
definitely want to be
alone.

41. Happiness
Do your best
to rule the world
happily.

42. Orders
Take orders,
carry them out properly
and be proud of the warrior,
you are a warrior.

43. Doer

I
have done
everything.

44. Miracle

There is no additional miracle,
the known should be
enough.

45. Frame

The frame has the beautiful framing
that the frame wants.

46. Happiness

I was happy,
couldn't see the sun
and was looking forward to silliness.

47. Slowly

Come back to your senses,
become a decent person,
strengthen your arms
and let views play for pleasure.

48. Imagination

If you think a lot to stimulate your
imagination,
be sure to look ahead
and improve yourself.

49. Weekend
Find everything on the weekend,
New Year,
without effort.

50. Noise
The constant sound in the small head is
music,
sound,
sound and good for everyone.

51. Number
Pay everything,
do not leave bills unpaid,
gifts are dangerous,
happiness is a heavy penalty.

52. Abbreviations
Shortcuts are so common that in the
long run
there is no shortcut to find a way out.

53. Number
It is well calculated,
intelligent,
well calculated
and still shaded,
but it is still a new beginning.

54. Words
There will always
be the word life.

55. Rest
The rest is open,
the rest is back,
everything else is everywhere,
needs some space
and everything is open.

56. Completed
Prepare now,
have the pleasure of thinking every day
without thinking too much.

57. Vanity
Seize vanity,
lose your sight
and fall.

58. Light
And it comes to light,
and many believe
that they can be infected.

59. Eclipse
Have seen the plan
and think the day well,
sentences invert the world,
just come through it
and be there.

60. Wrung out
Well wrung out the construct,
catch the good inventions of life.

Today I was with my son in the city and ate an ice cream with him. That was really good. The togetherness. The ice cream and the hustle and bustle in the city. My son is autistic and can rarely wait. When I stand in the long line to buy the ice cream, he waits patiently. This is a great exception. Waiting can be nice.

61. Games
Reinvent old games,
feel briefly secure
and talk to yourself.

62. Rain
The raindrop sticks to the glass,
the thoughts stick to life with the
raindrop
and meet you.

63. Illusion
The illusion of knowledge narrows my
good work breaks
and I breathe.

64. Attitude
Fine sounds emerge from the noises
and the attitude gets an additional
narrowing
and the morning sun warms.

65. Reason
A very good reason to live
is to know better without being caught,
by oneself or by others.

66. Nose
Orientation by the nose
helps to get to the destination
and to die.

67. Watch out
The smell on the fingers
opens a new world
and captures.

68. Without
Especially the word without has great
content
and likes to take us
to the beginning into an innocent
world
and turns us around.

69. Useful
Useful is good to us
and must not be lost until the end.

70. Finite

Finite takes us into an infinity,
let us examine opinions,
gladly we just adopt them.

71. Condition

The good condition of the neglected
shocks
and makes us think,
because performance counts
and then I may.

72. Sun

Innocently
the sun penetrates the sunburn.

73. Blooming
Briefly the old man blossoms,
looks into the merry circle
and takes the last train home,
all seems well.

74. Desolate
The fish is already stinking
and the hungry
are impatiently scolding you.

75. Buds
Excited,
everyone runs blindly to their doom,
breathing short and aging fast.

76. Leg-hard
Currently you must be leg-hard
and endure much torment,
so you can go to heaven
and finally be happy.

77. Initially
The train left in the beginning,
no one heard a sound,
it hasn't been so quiet for ages
and again in the beginning.

78. Unfounded
To have forgotten everything
and to be accused unfoundedly
friendly.

79. Gear
Travelling long distances
and arriving at the thoughts of others,
breaking up and dividing
and sliding away.

80. Sense
In turning around
lies buried a great mystery
and remains unknown.

81. Hand
Squeeze the enemy's hand without
strength
and give up life and happiness suddenly
comes flying and create.

82. Glass
The breaking glass remained in the
mind,
no one expected the end now.

83. Food
Quickly gulp down the food
and be an epicure,
more makes the right to be an epicure
and distinguishes.

84. Liberation
Out of weariness go to church
and with the scratching thoughts hope
for the final liberation,
well done.

85. Again
Again and again
the good righteous appear disgustingly
unrighteous.

86. Alien
Not being at home in the garden,
hoping in the extraterrestrial the
explanation for today,
taking all mysticism in the plastic bag.

87. Punctual
Wearing the right shirt at the right time
and getting to the funeral on time.

88. Dreamy
Fly dreamily through the air,
breathe in the scent of other people,
wash myself
and be a dreamer of the best kind.

89. Heroes
Since I got a medal,
I can now call myself
a human being.

90. High
The clouds in the sky seem to fly quite
high,
know by heart the past,
be a decal and laugh.

Many poems in this book are inspired by people with autism and by people who have no ordinary consciousness, or are simply mentally always somewhere else, not here in our commonly imagined world. At least that's how one imagines it. Is there an ordinary, common world?

91. Any

For good reasons,
the driver could not stop,
any responsibility was on the others,
and love was also a word.

92. Quickly

The bird on the window
sill chirps my morning song way too
fast.

93. Out

How far still go out to be high,
play with life and become more
and be higher,
have done well.

94. Responsibility

I'll give you the responsibility,
it's really none of my business,
just like you.

95. Worm

The worm
has found your hole of thoughts
and finds a home here
and stays with you
for the rest of your life.

96. Heart

With an empty heart I meet my heart,
with an empty heart I meet your heart,
with an empty heart I meet being.

Part 2

We come to the 2nd part. Further 96
poems follow. Some poems resemble
each other and are spun on in the
following associated poem or also
dissolved. In the whole book always 3
poems belong together. However,
these were well mixed by me. It is not
necessary to go consciously on the
search. By chance one will come across
it, or not.

97. Prison
Having life locked up
very securely
in the prison of dreams.

98. Love
In the thirst for love forget the self,
think good
and ask.

99. Ask
And we ask and pray,
poetry stories
and again be in the prison of dreams,
in the prison of love.

100. Morning

A good morning brings back hope,
a good day makes you forget dying for
a moment,
it will be a good day.

101. Born again

Being born again and again,
dying again and again.

102. Fear

Fear has postponed you,
the good days are not over.

103. Fear free
Fear or fear-free,
spring will come,
to you and to me.

104. Crosses
The two crosses stood on the
mountain
and in me,
carry more than one cross,
lose hope or the crosses.

105. Firm
We hold eternally to the crosses,
they also give an inverted sense.

106. Emptiness

Finally found the emptiness
and suddenly discover the crosses
again,
they begin to curse and be determined.

107. Wound

Not letting the wound of the heart
heal,
taking care of the wound properly
and letting everything into the heart,
poison and waste.

108. Unfortunately

Unfortunately,
the suffering does not always have a
great meaning,
but for the displacement,
the suffering always makes sense.

While I was putting the pages together, I thought about decorating the book with pictures. A few times I did that, then I deleted the pictures again. With the cover picture, it was easy. The image is the reflection in the kitchen cabinet from the dining set at my house. I digitally processed the image. In total, I made a series of 24 images from the base image. I used another image from this series as the cover image in the volume "Poetry".

109. Trust
Take confidence in thoughts
and make a solid image out of it.

110. Solidified
The wave hits me
and I realize the solid in me,
protected dull.

111. Sound
The sounding absolute silence has hit
you briefly
and disappears with the first thought of
success.

112. Despondent
Change despondency into success
consciousness
and be strong
and win
and kill
and finally be human.

113. Excited
Excited is not excited
and does not come from somewhere,
but has something to do with
unreasonableness
and invades spontaneously.

114. Candle
Standing candle-straight
and thinking of straight
and of the candle,
thinking of incredible cheerfulness
and being straight.

115. Apple
I found the apple,
but is already something rotten at the
core.

116. Vomit
The vomit of the friendly drunk smells
sour
and drives away my love of wholeness
and understanding.

117. Dandruff
The shoulders full of hair dandruff
somewhat dampens the feigned
superiority.

118. Brakes
You brake me with your superiority
and I just keep dreaming of great
possessions
and I'll show you already.

119. Up
When the door opened
and the great sage entered,
he stumbled stupidly.

120. Friendly
To be kind again
and to embrace the world worldly
and be mastered.

121. Core
The great difference in the core shows
everyone
that there is no difference at all,
we reproduce and die.

122. Saying
The good sentence and the good saying
invite you to sit and fly away.

123. Balanced
Well balanced sit on the earth
and laugh and lost again,
how is it right,
when you have you again.

124. Hoarfrost

To be very ripe
and to be very rough,
to have lost the beginning
and you give yourself the order to find
the beginning again.

125. Load

The load moves into the earth,
deeper and deeper,
the earth is waiting for you.

126. Sounds

Permeated by the sounds,
by the loud
and even louder sounds
and think
and finally say something clever.

127. Exchange
Exchanging some things,
fluids and thoughts,
feelings and hard knowledge,
beliefs and stubbornness
and oneself.

128. Jumped off
Once more and once more
and then run away or not.

129. Short
Looking at the sun,
of course,
briefly and kindly,
although that already hurts,
praising the sun,
briefly and very kindly.

If you come across this thought, may I share my thought with you. I was just wondering where you are, how you feel when you read the poems and who you are?

130. Net
Wets the thinkers to examine for
explanations,
for the right sense.

131. Brutal
Without consideration drink the last sip
and like to be brutal,
this is a timeless good character trait.

132. Promised
Not having promised anything
and creating the center of the earth in
spite of herd consciousness,
come here and surrender.

133. Admonisher

Slowly the admonitions of the
admonisher fade,
the admonisher has become old
and thin,
emaciated he seems.

134. Reason

There is no real reason
to accumulate great knowledge.

135. Doing

To be completely out of one's mind,
to want to be there for sure,
and to be connected.

136. Happiness
A luck to be there
and to have control over the worlds,
good luck.

137. Order
Getting an order,
carrying it out properly
and being proud like a warrior,
you must be a warrior.

138. Appearance
Stepped up and kicked it all in,
be the exemplary strong one.

139. Miracle

There are no additional miracles after
all,
the known ones must suffice.

140. Frame

The frame has a beautiful framing
function,
framing hope.

141. Seeing

I couldn't see the sun for luck,
and I rejoiced foolishly.

142. Slowly
Coming back to my senses
and being a tidy person,
strengthening arms
and flexing muscles for joy.

143. Twisted
Have thought too much
and twist the conceit,
nod and affirm,
affirm and think on,
make good.

144. Weekend
A weekend,
an end of year and an end of life,
find everything,
without effort.

145. Noise

The continuous noise in the small head
has become music,
a hiss and clang and be friendly to all,
be good.

146. Pay

All may pay,
no bill remains unpaid,
gifts are dangerous
and happiness will be a bad
punishment.

147. Abbreviation

Since the shortcut became habit,
there is no shortcut,
see an arduous life
through the long ways.

148. Miscalculated
To have calculated well,
to be a clever head,
to have calculated well
and yet miscalculated
and yet a new beginning.

149. Words
There will always be words,
words describing
the whole life.

150. Opened
The rest has opened up,
the restlessness comes again
and everything else is all around,
takes hardly any space,
open up everything.

151. Ready
Being ready now,
doing the work
and having earned the pleasure through
it,
every day new without thinking much.

152. Vanity
Grab you by the vanity
and already lost,
fall down.

153. Shine
And it shines the head,
many believe that they can catch.

154. Love
Love must not be forgotten here,
the one love and the other love,
the imagined love
and the emptied love.

155. Darkness
If you look closely at the plan
and think about the day,
the statement will be spread all over the
world.

156. Exposure
Well,
I found a good invention of life
and wrote down its composition.

My world is small, often thoughtless
and often without hope. And suddenly
everything blossoms and I am
permeated with good thoughts. Then I
think to myself again what thoughts
can do.

157. Game
Reinvent the old game,
feel safe
and talk to each other.

158. Rain
The raindrops stick to the glass
and the idea sticks to the living
raindrops
and attacks you.

159. Illusion
The illusion of realization limits my
good work to be interrupted,
I breathe.

160. Attitude
The tone is subtle,
the attitudes tighten
and the morning sun warms up.

161. Reason
A very good reason to live
is to know better without being caught
by oneself or others.

162. Nose
The direction
to the nose helps to reach
the goal
and die.

163. Perceive
The smell of the finger
opens a new world.

164. None
Especially the word "none" has a great
content,
so I would like to consider the
beginning of an innocent world.

165. Convenience
Convenience is a good intention
and will not be lost until the end.

166. Finite

Finite takes us infinitely
and let us reconsider our opinions,
we will gladly accept them.

167. Condition

Performance is important
and then allowed,
so I think a good shock condition
will be ignored.

168. Sun

The sun innocently penetrates
the sunburn.

169. Prosperity

The old man blossoms for a moment,
looks happy,
comes home on the last train,
all seems well.

170. Kill

The fish already stinks
and is hungry.

171. Running

Excited,
everyone runs blindly,
exhales and ages prematurely.

172. Heart
Now you are hard
and have to endure so much pain
that you can finally go to heaven
and be happy.

173. Beginning
The train was lost at first,
no one heard noise,
it was not very quiet for years
and at first.

174. Fact free
I forgot everything
and received an unfounded friendly
request.

175. Speed
Move long distances
until you reach the other person's
head.

176. Sense
The rotation reveals a great mystery
and remains unknown.

177. Hand
If you cling to the enemy's hand
and give up your life without violence,
luck will fly.

178. Glass
The broken glass remained in the idea
and no one expected the end.

179. Food
Get ready to eat,
become an enthusiast,
give more rights to enthusiasts
and great people.

180. Cancel
It was not boring to go to church
and wish something
with the vague idea of the last view.

181. Still
Often righteous people
look uncomfortable
and unjust.

182. Alien
Not in the garden house,
put all secrets in plastic bags
and count on aliens.

183. Right
Wear the right shirt at the right time
and arrive on time for the funeral.

184. Dream
Like the dreams flying in the sky,
the best kind of dream is to wash
myself
and breathe the smell of others.

185. Heroes
After receiving the medals,
I can call myself a human being.

186. High
Clouds of the sky seem to fly high,
remembering the past
and laughing with decals.

187. Arbitrary
For good reasons,
the driver could not stop,
every responsibility was with others,
even love was a word.

188. Fast
Birds at the window sing a song
early in the morning.

189. Out
Go, go up,
play in life, go up, go up, go well,
do well.

190. Responsibility
I'll give you the responsibility,
it's not my job at all.

191. Worms
Worms find holes in your mind,
find their home here
and stay with you
for the rest of your life.

192. Heart
I meet my heart,
I meet your heart
with an empty heart,
I meet my presence
with an empty heart.

Part 3

In the previous two parts, you may
have noticed that all thoughts are
repetitive. So it is also with my other
work, everything repeats itself, repeats
itself almost without end. Just like the
heartbeat. Not exciting, but necessary.
And at some point there is an end. But
until the end we should be alive.

193. Prison

You are confined to trauma prisons
with very limited life.

194. Love

For love,
I forget myself,
question and think.

195. Petition

And we pray to be in the prison of
love,
in the dark history
and again in the prison of dreams.

196. Morning
In the good morning
I remember hope
and forget a good day,
it will be a good day.

197. Reborn
The thought is reborn again and again
and dies again and again.

198. Fear
Fear has impressed you,
a good day is not over.

199. Do not worry
Spring comes to you with me,
whether you are afraid or not.

200. Cross
The two crosses stood in the
mountains
and in me,
carrying one or more crosses,
lost,
hope and crosses.

201. Celebration
We cling to the cross forever,
we give false meanings again.

202. Heaven
When you finally find the gap
and suddenly discover the cross,
begin to curse
and decide.

203. Scratch
Heal wounds of the heart,
properly care for the wounds,
leave nothing in the heart,
poisons or garbage.

204. Unfortunately
Unfortunately,
suffering does not always have a great
purpose,
but it always makes sense.

205. Trust
Please
draw a solid picture with confidence
in your idea.

206. Solidification
When the waves hit me,
I noticed the fire inside me.

207. Sound
A resounding absolute silence hits you
for a moment
and disappears at the first thought of
success.

208. Discouraged
It turns discouragement into a sense of
achievement,
becomes stronger,
wins,
kills,
and finally becomes human.

209. Excitement
Excitement is not excited,
it does not come from anywhere,
it attacks spontaneously
when everything becomes impossible.

210. Candle
Stand up
straight and think of the incredible
calmness
of the candle.

211. Apple
I found the apple,
but the core is a little rotten.

212. Vomit
Friendly vomit smells sour
and destroys my love of wholeness
and understanding.

213. Dandruff
Damp shoulders slightly weakened
the benefits of the game.

214. Brake
They slow me down with their
superiority,
and I always dream of great things,
and I show you.

215. Up
When the door opened
and a great king entered,
he was stupid
and stumbled.

216. Friendly
Become kind again,
accept the world
and rule the world.

In between once find rest, then start
running again and get out of breath.
Being hungry, getting drunk and loving
a lot. Helping others and being happy
in the process.

217. Core
The great difference at the core shows everyone
that there is no difference at all.

218. Say
If you have good phrases or proverbs,
I suggest you sit down
and fly away.

219. Balanced
I sat balanced on the floor
and laughed and died again,
when will you come back?

220. Frost
Please give me the task of being very
mature
and very rough,
losing the beginning
and finding the beginning.

221. Finally
The load goes deep into the earth
and the earth is waiting for you.

222. Sound
The sound is drenched,
loud,
thinks
and says something wise at the end.

223. Love

Remember the love here,
the love of one and the other,
the caring love
and the love of heaven.

224. Darkness

After looking at the plan
and thinking about the day,
the proposals go through the world.

225. Construct

Now,
they have overcome the construct
and captured the good inventions of
life.

226. Game
Invent old games,
feel safe
and communicate with each other.

227. Rain
The raindrop sticks to the glass,
the thoughts stick together with the
living drop
and meet you.

228. Illusion
The illusion of consciousness restricts
my good work
and I breathe.

229. Adjustment
Sounds come from the sounds of
subtle sounds,
the situation narrows,
the morning sun heats up.

230. Reason
A very good reason to live
is to know better
and not to be caught by you or others.

231. Nose
Concentrating on the nose
helps to reach the goal
and die.

232. Observing
The smell on your fingers
opens a new world
and it begins.

233. Without
Especially the word without has great
content
and takes us to the beginning of the
innocent world
and turns around.

234. Useful
It can be used with good intentions
and cannot be lost until the end.

235. Finally
Parts take us to the infinite,
let's check the opinions,
we gladly accept them.

236. Condition
The good condition of the broken
stamps makes us think,
because performance is considered
and then allowed.

237. Sun
The sun innocently passes
into a sunburn.

238. Flourish
The old man blossoms briefly,
looks cheerful,
gets on the last train home,
everything seems fine.

239. Sad
The fish already stinks
and hunger is filled with impatience for
us.

240. Old
Excited,
everyone is running blindly,
breathing fast
and getting old quickly.

Are you okay? Are you missing
something for happiness? When will
the end come? Do you still have some
time?

241. Leg-hard
Right now you have to be strong
and suffer so you can go to heaven
and finally be happy.

242. In the beginning
In the beginning,
the train was lost,
no one heard the sound,
it was not so quiet and first.

243. Unreasonable
All the accused have forgotten
and are unreasonable friends.

244. Travel
Travel long distances
and come to the thoughts of others,
break,
share and run away.

245. Meaning
The sentence reveals a great secret
and remains unknown.

246. Hand
Squeeze the enemy's hand without
strength
and give up life,
and good luck flies to,
manage everything well.

247. Glass
Shards of glass stuck in memory,
no one expected the end now.

248. Food
Throw away food
and become an epicure,
more pleasure and enjoyment.

249. Release
Go to church out of boredom
and think about the final redemption
with determined thoughts.

250. Again
Again and again
the good righteous
seem to be disgusting and unfair.

251. Alien
Not at home in the garden,
hoping to explain it to the aliens
and stealthily hiding the secret.

252. Punctual
Wear the right shirt at the right time
and be on time for the funeral.

253. Dreamy
Dreamily fly through the air,
breathe in other people's smells
and become a better-looking dreamer.

254. Heroes
Since I received a medal,
I can call myself a man.

255. High
The clouds in the sky seem to fly high,
remember the past,
you are a sticker
and laugh.

256. Arbitrary
The driver could not resist,
all the responsibility fell on others,
and even love was a word.

257. Fast
The bird on the windowsill
chirps the morning song too fast.

258. Out
How far from being,
being big,
playing with life,
becoming more
and more and doing well.

259. Responsibility
I hold you responsible,
it's none of my business
how you are.

260. Worm
The worm has found a hole in your
mind,
has found a home here
and will stay with you
until the end of your life.

261. Heart
With an empty heart I meet my heart,
with an empty heart I meet your heart,
with an empty heart I meet a being.

262. Prison
Life in a dream
cage is very limited.

263. Love
Forget yourself in the thirst for love,
think carefully and ask.

264. Inquiries
We pray
and pray with stories to be back in the
prison of dreams,
to be in the prison of love.

265. Morning
Good morning returns hope,
a good day will make you die,
it will be a good day.

266. Born again
To be born again and again,
to be dead again and again.

267. Fear
Fear has touched you,
the good days are not over yet.

268. Without fear
Be fearful or fearless,
spring will come for you
and for me.

269. Crosses
Two crosses stood on a mountain
and in me,
they carried more than one cross
and lost hopes or crosses.

270. Festival
We always hold on to crosses,
they also give the wrong meaning.

271. Emptiness
When you find emptiness
and unexpectedly find crosses,
you start cursing
and will be decisive.

272. Hardened
The wave beats me
and I notice the feast inside me,
protected by the mutes.

273. Sound
The sounding absolute silence hit you
and disappeared with the first thought
of success.

Slowly it comes to an end. But probably no reader will have started from the beginning. Probably not you either. And that's just as well. You don't always start from the beginning. You just jump into the unknown and you get going.

274. Discouraged
Turn sadness into a feeling of success
and be strong,
conquer and kill
and finally become a human being.

275. Excited
Excited is not excited
and does not come from anywhere,
has to do with intelligence
and spontaneous attacks.

276. Candle
Just get up
and think clearly
and by candlelight,
think of incredible happiness
and just rest.

277. Apple
I found an apple,
but the apple was rotten.

278. Vomit
Friendly drunken vomit smells sour
and dissipates my love for honesty
and understanding.

279. Dandruff
The scales on the shoulders
easily weaken the superiority
in the game.

280. Drakes
You brake me with your superiority,
and I always dream of great
possessions,
and I will show you.

281. Wise
When the door opened
and the great sage entered,
he stumbled stupidly.

282. Kind
Be kind,
accept
and rule the world again.

283. Core
The great difference in the core
shows everyone that there is no
difference,
we plant and die.

284. Suggestion
A good suggestion
and a good saying invite you
to sit down
and fly away.

285. Balanced
Sit down well on the ground,
laugh and lose again,
how right is it
when you return?

286. Frost
Be very mature
and very rude,
lost the beginning
and set ourselves the task of finding
the beginning.

287. Last
The burden pulls you
deeper and deeper into the earth,
the earth is waiting for you.

288. Sound
Permeated by sounds,
by soft and loud sounds,
think
and finally say something wise.

End. A happy ending. Hopefully.